PRIMARY READERS
STARTERS

The Magic Carpet

Brendan Dunne
Robin Newton

Illustrator: Pedro Penizotti

The Johnson family are moving house.

The twins are reading.

LOOK AT THE CARPET! WHAT IS IT DOING?

The twins fly fast and win the race.

The twins see their carpet and they're happy. They have one more wish.